Fabulous FASHIONs of the 1940s

FELICIA
LOWENSTEIN
NIVEN

Fabulous FASHIONs of the DECADES

E Enslow Publishers, Inc.
40 Industrial Road
Box 398
Berkeley Heights, NJ 07922
USA

http://www.enslow.com

Library of Congress Cataloging-in-Publication Data
Niven, Felicia Lowenstein.
    Fabulous fashions of the 1940s / Felicia Lowenstein Niven.
        p. cm. — (Fabulous fashions of the decades)
    Fabulous fashions of the nineteen forties
    Includes bibliographical references and index.
    Summary: "Discusses the fashions of the 1940s, including women's and men's clothing and hair-
       styles, accessories, trends and fads, and world events that influenced the fashion"—Provided by
       publisher.
    ISBN 978-0-7660-3552-2
    1. Fashion—History—20th century—Juvenile literature. 2. Fashion design—History—20th cen-
    tury—Juvenile literature. 3. Lifestyle—History–20th century—Juvenile literature. 4. Nineteen
    forties—Juvenile literature. I. Title. II. Title: Fabulous fashions of the nineteen forties.
      TT504.N57 2011
      746.9'20904—dc22
      2010004195

Paperback ISBN: 978-1-59845-277-8

Printed in the United States of America

052011 Lake Book Manufacturing, Inc., Melrose Park, IL

10 9 8 7 6 5 4 3 2 1

To Our Readers: We have done our best to make sure all Internet Addresses in this book
were active and appropriate when we went to press. However, the author and the publisher
have no control over and assume no liability for the material available on those Internet sites
or on other Web sites they may link to. Any comments or suggestions can be sent by e-mail to
comments@enslow.com or to the address on the back cover.

Every effort has been made to locate all copyright holders of material used in this book. If any
errors or omissions have occurred, corrections will be made in future editions of this book.

♻ Enslow Publishers, Inc., is committed to printing our books on recycled paper. The paper
in every book contains 10% to 30% post-consumer waste (PCW). The cover board on the
outside of each book contains 100% PCW. Our goal is to do our part to help young people
and the environment too!

Contents

The 1940s

This page from a 1943 Sears® catalog shows different brands of leg makeup. It was an interesting alternative to actual stockings. It was applied using a makeup sponge or powder puff, just like foundation.

Platforms are high fashion for Spring

High soles are high fashion
$3.69

J   Exciting version of a favorite South American fashion note. Bow makes your foot look smaller. Fine crushed kid or patent leather. 2½-inch Cuban heel.
• A (very narrow) width in sizes 5 to 9.
C (med.) width in women's sizes 4 to 9. All half sizes, too. State size and width.
$5 E 8027—White crushed kid
$5 E 8026—Black patent leather
Shipping weight, 1 lb. 3 oz. . . . . . Pair $3.69

Port hole perforations
$3.69

H   Fine, sleek patent or soft crushed kid. Neat bow. Cushiony platform. Leather soles 2½-in. Cuban heels.
• A (very narrow) only in sizes 5 to 9.
C (medium) in women's sizes 4 to 9. Half sizes, too. State size width.
$5 E 8024—Beige crushed kid
$5 E 8025—White crushed kid
$5 E 8023—Black patent leather
Shipping weight, 1 lb. 3 oz. . . . . . Pair $3.69
◆Means sent from Chicago. Order, pay postage from nearest mail order house.

Leg Make-up for that silk stocking glamour

Ann Barton Leg Make-up—Lotion type
Save precious hose—wear liquid make-up in place of stockings. Easily, quickly applied with powder puff, cotton, sponge, or smoothed on with the hands. Gives legs a smooth sheer, stocking-like appearance. Does not rub off on clothes. Light Suntan or Dark Suntan. May be removed with soap and warm water. State shade.
8 E 5774—4-ounce bottle. Postpaid 39c

Harriet Hubbard Ayer Stocking Lotion
Lasting. Easily applied—goes on without streaking; dries rapidly—gives legs a golden sun-tan finish.
8 E 5141—4-ounce bottle. Postpaid 39c

Patrick's Leg Art—Liquid Dye type
Use Patrick's Leg Art. Three popular shades: Beige (light), Copper (medium), Rust (dark). State shade.
8 E 5986—3-ounce bottle $1.10

Leg Charm—Cream type
For a smooth silk stocking effect. Applies just like cold cream. Run-proof wrinkle-free "sheer-silk" leg make-up. State shade: Nude or Sun Tan.
8 E 3152—3½ ounce bottle 41c

Helena Rubinstein—Leg Stick
Easy to apply. Gives legs a sun tan appearance.
8 E 5963—Postpaid 52c

Ann Barton Cake Make-up (not shown)
Stays on a long time—easily applied with moistened puff or sponge. Convenient to carry in cosmetic bag or purse. Comes in Tulle Mist (light), Ivory Satin (medium), or Heirloom Lace (dark). State shade.
8 E 5988—¾ ounce. Plastic case. Postpaid . . . 39c

Max Factor Pan-Cake make-up
Used by the stars in Hollywood for greater leg appeal. Lends a smooth, silky appearance to your legs. Easy, quick to apply. Natural No. 1, Natural-Rose Cream No. 1, Tan No. 1. State shade wanted.
8 E 4215—1½ ounce. Postpaid $1.65

Elmo Photo-Finish Make-up (not shown)
Sponge on in a jiffy—gives a sheer stocking-like appearance . . . lasts for hours. Nude (light), Peach (medium), and Copper (dark). State shade.
8 E 5505—1¼ ounce. Postpaid $1.65

Solitair—by Campana (not shown)
Filmy loveliness for your legs. Contains lanolin. Natural (lgt.), Rachel, Peach Bloom, Brunette, Golden Tan (med.), Bronze (dk.).
8 E 3608—¾ ounce. Postpaid. State shade 66c

Large Puffs . . for leg or cake make-up (not shown)
Double thick cotton puffs, especially absorbent.
8 E 4174—Shpg. wt. 3 oz. . . . . 10 puffs for 10c

Wild and Crazy Fads

When you get dressed up, you might put on a pair of nylon stockings. Nylon was a relatively new invention in 1940. But American women did not get too used to wearing it. That was because nylon was needed to make parachutes for war. Silk was used, too. It was hard to find silk or nylon stockings.

So women did something imaginative. They "painted" on their stockings. Women used leg makeup like Cyclax Stockingless Cream. Then they carefully drew the stocking seams down the backs of their legs with eyebrow pencils. Some women even used cocoa or brown gravy to color their legs like stockings. Now that was a crazy fad!

Teenage and younger girls did not always take the time to paint on stockings. Instead, they wore the ankle socks that were popular in Britain. These were called bobby sox, after the slang word for British police officers. The style really set teenagers apart from adults. It would be popular for decades.

This issue of *Home Front* magazine came with a voucher for a free paper pattern. You could have used the material from clothes you did not wear anymore to make something completely new!

6

Introduction: Wild and Crazy Fads

Everybody got used to doing without things in the 1940s. A popular World War II poster featured the saying, "Use it up. Wear it out. Make it do."

It was one reason that the McCall Pattern Company introduced a new kind of sewing pattern. The pattern changed men's suits into women's suits and women's dresses into children's clothing. Talk about a family resemblance!

Hats were popular during this time. It was a way to change a look without buying new clothes. Of course, hatmakers did not always have the right materials. After all, it was wartime and hard to get some things. So when they ran out of felt, feathers, and tulle, they got creative. They used braided paper, cellophane, and even wood shavings!

These were just some of the wild and crazy fads of the 1940s. Read on to find out more about this colorful decade.

During the 1940s, many materials used in fashion had to be redirected to the soldiers fighting in World War II. People had to get creative to keep in style. For example, accessorizing with a beret, brooch, and gloves made a simple black suit look extra glamorous!

Chapter 1

Hairstyles

It was wartime. That affected how women wore their hair, and not only women in uniform. War meant shortages. It was hard to get hairpins and hats. So the most popular styles did not use them. But that wasn't the only effect that war had on hair.

Most men were fighting for our country. Therefore, women took over their jobs in factories. Women with long hair had a problem because their hair could get caught in the machines. The workers could get badly injured if that happened.

So women chose shorter styles or put their hair up. The funny part is that women were told they were helping their country by choosing these styles. The styles were considered patriotic! They were even named that way, such as the victory roll and the liberty cut.

Aside from hair being up and out of the way, there were plenty of curls. Curls appeared in many hairstyles of the era. Women wore them whether they had curly hair or not. Women spent hours setting their hair at night to get the perfect curly or wavy look.

"V" for Victory Rolls

Victory rolls were easy, and they worked on all hair types. To create a victory roll, a woman took a section of hair at the front, rolled it away from her face, and pinned it there. The rolls could be large or small. Women liked their hair to have height and would pin the rolls on top of their heads.

Actress and dancer Ginger Rogers (1911–1995) styled her hair in victory rolls in 1949. She and Fred Astaire starred in several popular musicals of the 1930s.

Hairstyles

They could then leave the rest of their hair down or pin that up, too. Victory rolls were an elegant look, great for both everyday and fancier occasions.

Freedom of the Liberty Cut

The liberty cut was very practical. It only needed to be cut once every three months. Hair was clipped to a few inches from the head. Then it was curled and styled. It was easy to do at home and required very few pins because of the length of the hair.

Knot It in a Chignon

The chignon, or soft bun, was one of the more popular hairstyles. The bun was pinned at the nape of the neck, making it easy for women to keep their hair out of the way. Factory workers wore it with a headscarf. It was also easy to make it look fancy. In fact, many teenagers today will wear a chignon to a prom or other event.

Cooking Up an Omelet Fold

The omelet fold looked a little like the breakfast food for which it was named. It involved parting the hair in the back. Then a woman crossed the two sides, bringing them up toward the top. If she did it right, the back looked like she had folded over an omelet. The hair ended up at the top of the head in a mass of pin curls.

Jazz singer Ella Fitzgerald (1917–1996) wore her hair in a pretty omelet fold with curls cascading down the front of her head in this 1949 picture. Women from all different ethnic backgrounds sported curls.

Chapter 2

Women's Styles and Fashion

Everyone recognized Paris, France, as the center of the fashion world. In wartime, that all changed. When the Germans invaded the city in 1940, they took over. The Parisian designers worked for them. Communication with the rest of the world became difficult. Few people saw the new Paris fashions.

Some designers closed their shops. Others changed their designs to suit German tastes. This was not good for the European fashion industry. But in America, it opened up a door. American designers had the opportunity to influence fashion.

They had to work around some rules, though. In 1942, the government limited the amount and types of fabric that could be used in clothing. For example, leather was needed for soldiers' boots, and silk was needed for parachutes.

That started a whole new style, the utility style, which was practical and basic. There was not a lot of material used. Skirts and jackets became shorter. Designers might skip pockets or cuffs. At night, women wore sheaths instead of long, flowing evening gowns.

The war influenced fashion in other ways. The military look was popular. Many suits and dresses were tailored like uniforms. They had sharp boxy shoulders. Necks were high cut with small collars. Details such as breast pockets and belts created a uniform look.

Because of wartime, it became acceptable for women to wear the same styles for much longer. Magazines gave hints on how to care for dresses and suits so they would last. Separates were popular. Women mixed skirts and tops to make it seem as if their wardrobes were larger than they actually were.

After the war, women were ready for a change. They were tired of the tailored military look. They wanted more feminine designs. That opened the way for designers such as Christian Dior, who created long and full skirts and a more feminine look. Pleated designs became especially popular. They used more fabric and allowed for fuller skirts.

One popular full style was the shirtwaist dress. It was the female version of the man's flannel gray suit, the kind of classic outfit that every woman had in her closet. The shirtwaist dress looked a little like a man's shirt. It had a similar collar. It could be long- or short-sleeved. It was often belted or tied at the waist. This allowed the skirt to flare out in a full style. The shirtwaist dress was so popular that it appeared both in casual materials for daytime and fancier materials for evening.

March It Out in Military Style

The military style was very popular in clothes of the 1940s. It was practical and did not use a lot of extra material. Dresses had square shoulders. Skirts were narrowed or slightly flared. They came to just below the knee. There was not a lot of decoration, such as ruffles. After all, there was a fabric shortage.

Wearing the Pants in the Family

Up until the 1940s, not too many women had dared to wear pants. But that all changed. Women put on jeans, known then as dungarees. They wore one-piece denim coveralls, or overalls. These were popular outfits for working at a factory.

As fashions became casual, hair and makeup became more important. Women looked feminine in pants because of their curls and bright lipstick.

A woman works on a plane motor in 1942. She has her hair up in a victory roll and tied back with a bandana to keep it from getting caught in dangerous machinery. She also wears jeans and a short-sleeved shirt for comfort and safety.

Shorter and Slinkier

Evening gowns required many yards of fabric. Because that wasn't available in the 1940s, women found an alternative. It was elegant and simple and didn't need a lot of fabric. It was the figure-hugging sheath, which came in at the waist without the need for a belt or waistband. Because it didn't need special decorations, it was perfect for wartime.

SIZE SCALE FOR SEPARATE SLACKS						
Order Size	12	14	16	18	20	
If waist is	25½	27	28½	30	32	in.
If hips are	35	36½	38	39½	41	in.

COTTON SLACKS . . washables for work or everyday

$1.59 $1.59

Just because women started wearing pants did not mean they had lost their femininity. These models wear makeup and curly hairdos with slacks. Their look could be both practical and pretty!

Dior Goes With the Flow

World War II ended in 1945. After years of wearing the same styles, everyone was ready for a change. As in past years, designers would have a real effect on what people wore—from the very rich to the everyday man or woman.

Christian Dior took a chance with his 1947 collection, creating a look that was feminine and flowing. He designed dresses and full skirts that used yards of fabric. Waists appeared tiny because shoulders and hips were padded.

Christian Dior's "New Look" collection emphasized an hourglass figure. Padded shoulders and full skirts made waists appear dramatically smaller than they really were.

Dior's designs were part of the "New Look" that would take over the 1950s which emphasized hourglass figures. He would become popular all over the world for his designs.

The World's First Supermodel

She once described herself as "a good clothes hanger." But Lisa Fonssagrives was more than that. She was the first supermodel. Trained as a ballerina, she had the grace and figure that landed her on magazine covers. Her face was one that became known—as models are today.

Fashion as Art

American designer Charles James may have been a poor businessman, but he was a brilliant designer. He experimented with different shapes like a sculptor. He designed in practical flannels and tweeds for daytime. But he was most well known for his evening gowns in fancy fabrics. He also was very forward thinking. He designed a wraparound skirt and an early version of the modern padded jacket.

Jersey Girl

Designer Claire McCardell loved the feel of jersey material. She also liked cotton and denim. She used these fabrics and others to make clothes for the ordinary woman, but in an unusual way. She made them into eveningwear.

She also hated the wedge heels of the 1940s. They may have been "all the rage," but she preferred something more feminine. She designed ballet slippers with stronger soles that could be worn outdoors.

Normally, people would look to French designers for new ideas. But the war prevented many Europeans from creating style-setting trends. In a way, it was the war that allowed such designers as McCardell to become so popular. She and other designers may not have created ready-to-wear sportswear, but they brought it to a whole new—and elegant—level.

Chapter 3

Men's Styles and Fashion

The fabric shortage didn't only affect women. Men's suits in the 1940s lost their vests, pocket flaps, pleats, and pants cuffs. Anything that required extra material was gone. Men who were not in uniform did not want to be too flashy when they dressed. It was considered patriotic to dress plainly and practically.

Of course, once the war ended, so did the plain styles. Men's clothes became full-cut again. Jackets were longer, and pants were wider. Shirts, coats, and ties were much more colorful.

In California and Florida, men started wearing really colorful shirts. You may know them as Hawaiian shirts.

They had flowers and flames, and sometimes pictures of women. The war was over. It was clearly a time for celebration, and men's wardrobes showed it!

Fit to a "T"

When 11 million American men put on uniforms to go to war, they also put on military underwear. This included an undershirt with sleeves. Called a T-type shirt, it had a round neck and short sleeves. It was made of cotton.

This style soon replaced the sleeveless undershirt that had been popular. Because of its association with war, the T-shirt was seen as manly. After the war, the T-shirt would become part of everyday fashion for men, too—and decades later for women.

The Mysterious Wide-Brimmed Fedora

Men in the 1940s looked a little mysterious. That was because of a popular hat known as the fedora. This felt hat was pinched in the

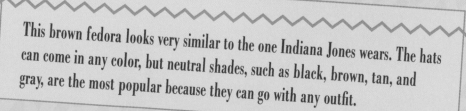

This brown fedora looks very similar to the one Indiana Jones wears. The hats can come in any color, but neutral shades, such as black, brown, tan, and gray, are the most popular because they can go with any outfit.

front but had a wide brim. It was the kind of hat that gangsters and detectives wore in movies. It is still popular today. You may have seen it on Britney Spears, Justin Timberlake, and Harrison Ford, who played Indiana Jones.

Jazz It Up With the Zoot Suit

Men's suits of the time were simply made. That was not the case with the zoot suit. This suit did not meet government recommendations. It used plenty of fabric and sported such details as pleats and cuffs.

These actors are dressed in zoot suits for a film in 1943. Zoot suits were banned during the war because they used too much material, but the government made an exception for the movie.

Zoot suits were usually worn in nightclubs. You would recognize it by the long jacket. Bulked up by six-inch shoulder pads, the jacket would go down to the knees. The pants were high around the waist. They were wide near the top but narrow by the ankles. The suit was worn with a wide-brimmed hat, slicked-back hair, and pointy shoes. A long watch chain, dangling from pocket to belt hook, completed the look.

Zoot suits were popular among young African-American and Mexican-American men. The suits became a symbol of ethnic pride. They also became the "uniform" for these young men when fights broke out between them and the white sailors and marines stationed in Los Angeles, California. The Zoot Suit Riots of 1943 called attention to the prejudice of the time.

Tie One On in Living Color

Almost every man wore ties back in the 1940s. Before World War II, those ties were in drab military colors. But after the war, there was an explosion of color. There were colorful geometric designs and hand-painted ones. There were pictures of favorite sports and movie stars! Men really started to express themselves through their neckwear.

At the best places...

And under the Christmas tree—you'll see the most popular white shirt in America—Arrow *Dart!* One reason for this out-size popularity: *the world's best-looking collar.* $3.65.

Arrow Shirts also boast the famous body-tapered fit (MITOGA trade-mark), and the Sanforized label (fabric shrinkage less than 1%). Other Arrow White Shirts—$3.65, $3.95, $4.50, $5.50 and $7.50.

For Christmas, give Arrow *Arabian Nights* ties! The designs are *extra*-handsome! (*Shown*) Fatima's Fan—and there are others equally striking, such as Aladdin's Lamp, the Dancing Doll, and Sinbad the Sailor. The fabric is a rich, luxurious rayon satin which knots and...though under the small...

ARROW SHIRTS and TIES

>>> Cluett, Peabody & Co., Inc.

An ad for Arrow® brand shirts and ties appears in the December 10, 1949, issue of the *Saturday Evening Post*. Postwar flashy ties were a welcome change to the dull designs found during World War II.

Chapter 4
Accessories

Accessories were very important during the 1940s. Women were limited in their wardrobe choices, so they used accessories to dress up plain outfits.

Hats were one accessory. They became smaller and more military during this decade. But they were not always available, so women turned to other ideas. Scarves and turbans were very popular. They protected women's hair when they worked in factories. Snoods, which were like knit hairnets, were also used to pull up long hair. Sometimes snoods were decorated with jewels or ribbons.

Women stopped wearing high heels because there were not a lot of them either. That was due to a shortage of leather.

Accessories

Because everything was hard to find, women often made their own accessories. They wore hand-knit scarves, winter gloves, and socks. They made their own underwear if they wanted something fancy. Old wedding dresses, pillowcases, and nightgowns were just some of the materials that became underwear.

Wrap It Up

In factories across America, hair was tied up in a colorful scarf or turban. Not only was this a feminine touch, but it was also a practical one! It kept the hair from being caught in the machinery. At home, scarves were also easy to wear when women did not feel like doing their hair. In many cases, the scarves and turbans replaced hats because they were cheaper and more available.

A Little Wedge Goes a Long Way

Do you own a platform shoe? You can thank French shoe designer Roger Vivier. He invented the modern platform in the 1930s. Of course, women had worn a form of platform shoes before that. That was back in the late 1500s when they had to keep their feet out of wet mud and garbage on the street.

The platform shoe had a wedge heel. This was a thick chunky heel. It also had a wedge sole. The whole foot was raised up several inches off the ground.

Turbans "Certain to Charm"

Cleverly Draped Fabrics...Fit Smooth...Look Trim...Colors to Brighten Any Wardrobe

"How To Measure" on First Hat Page

Nylon Sewn—Zelan Treated $1.59
A smart Turban that is made by hand with famous Nylon thread—this gives it elasticity... and we've Zelan processed the crush-resisting spun rayon to make it drape better... resist water and even ink stains! Wear it anytime without ever a worry about the weather! The casual styling plus Nylon sewing and the Zelan process make it a hat you'll wear and wear all year around. So flattering you're sure to receive compliments. We've priced it much less—even with all the features— than big city shops!
Colors: Black, Brown 219, Navy Blue, Dark Persian Rose 373, Red 313, Moss Green 825. Measure; state color wanted. Shipping weight, each, 14 ounces.
78 F 435—Fits 21¾ to 22¼-inch headsize.
78 F 436—Fits 22½ to 23 -inch headsize.

Rayon Velvet $1.59
A beautiful Turban that looks so expensive you'll never believe it could cost so little at Sears. You'll adore it to wear with your newest frocks. A gold-colored pin in the cent to a style that is smart and flattering. Favorite colors.
Colors: Black, Royal 569, Red 313, Mellow Amber 173, Moss Green 825. Measure; state color. Shipping weight, 14 ounces.
78 F 230—Fits 21¾ to 22¼-in. head.
78 F 231—Fits 22½ to 23-in. head.

Fan-Front Turban $1.39
Fashioned in lovely Rayon Velvet ... you'll wear it for "dress" and feel as elegant as the smart styling of the Turban. Snugs your head in back ... soars high in front in two fan-like bows that give you height and flatter your femininity. Remarkably low priced.
Colors: Black, Dark Brown 219, Navy Blue, Harvest Blue 659, Red Wine 367. Measure; state color wanted. Shipping wt., each, 14 oz.
78 F 315—Fits 21¾ to 22¼-in. head.
78 F 316—Fits 22½ to 23-in. head.

Special—Big Value $1.00
Softly draped with a flower-like cluster bunch at front to give you height and add a saucy accent to the styling. It fits superbly, too, because there's an elastic insert that "gives" to fit your head. Made of soft rayon Bagheera cloth. You'll find it practical and pretty for all occasions—for all types! You can have several at this price.
Colors: Black, Royal Blue 569, Rust 265 or Moss Green 825. Measure; state color. Shipping wt., 14 oz.
78 F 310—Fits 21¾ to 23-in. head.

2-way Turban $1.19
Wear the bow-cluster high in front or in a chignon low at the nape of your neck. It's smart either way ... and gives you two hats at the price of one! Soft Rayon Bagheera cloth of fine quality.
Colors: Black, Cadet Blue 621, Red 313, Vibrant Green 765, Mellow Amber 173. Measure; state color. Shpg. wt., 14 oz.
78 F 330—Fits 21¾ to 23-in. headsize.

Clever Wrap-around 69c
Of course it's becoming because you drape it to suit yourself! Goes round-and-back. In soft suede rayon you'll wear it neatly at front or with everything! You'll want more than one—the colors are grand!
Colors: Black, Harvest Rose 659, Dark Persian Rose 373, Brown 219, Gold Red 313, Navy Blue, Vibrant Green. State color wanted.
78 F ...

Pert Bustle Back $1.39
Lovely rayon velvet turban mode that combines the youthfulness of a Scottie style with the sophistication of a Pillbox. Bustle back is gracefully draped to add for all occasions. Rayon Velvet.

Veiled Halo Style
A lovely frame for your face. Off-the-face halo ...

There were many different styles of turbans in the 1940s. Many of them were quite fancy, such as these turbans from a Sears catalog. They had bows, intricate knots, flowers, decorative pins, bustles, and veils.

At the top are two of the many different styles of wedge heel shoes available at the time. On the left are pumps made out of perforated black leather. Next to them are spectator pumps. A spectator is a type of two-toned shoe that has a colored toe and heel, usually black, and a white middle. Wedges are still popular today, especially among younger women.

Best of all, the wedges could be made of cork or wood, which were easier materials than leather to get in wartime. Wooden clogs were noisy but practical. Cork shoes were very comfortable. Women could walk for miles on them without their feet getting sore. Both types lasted a long time and needed little repair.

Another Way to Milk It

When you need a new purse, you go to the store. But what if the store ran out of purses? If you were like the women in the 1940s, you might make your own.

Believe it or not, women made purses out of the lids from milk bottles. The bottles back then were very wide. The women covered the disks with raffia ribbon. They made them into pretty purses.

What's Under Your Clothes?

Early bras were used to flatten the chest. By the 1940s, the trend was the opposite. Bras were designed to show off a woman's shape. By the end of the decade, many were made with wire and padding.

In addition to bras, women wore panties and girdles, a type of elastic underwear that goes down to the thighs. It pushes everything in so a woman appears thinner. After the war, some of these styles got fancier. Designers combined nylon with stretchy panels and lace inserts.

No finer fit at any price

BESTFORM BRASSIERES
79¢
BESTFORM FOUNDATIONS
$2.50 to $6.50

BESTFORM
means "best form"

An advertisement for Bestform® bras from the 1940s. The waist-cinching designs of the 1940s made girdles unnecessary, but bras supported and brought attention to the bust.

Chapter 5

Fads and Trends

Everyone was preoccupied with war in the 1940s. The fads and trends of the era reflected that.

Women sewed their own clothes out of anything that was available, including parachutes, bedsheets, blankets, and other unusual materials. Knitting was a necessary skill during this time, and many people learned it.

The government also had a lot of say in how people dressed. Their rules kept Americans looking very much the same. They wore the same type of shoes—the only kind available. They wore the same types of dresses, pants, skirts, and coats. In fact, because there was not a lot that was new, they probably wore the very same outfits for years!

Hide It in the Kangaroo Cloak

The kangaroo cloak was a creation of wartime. Named for its huge kangaroo pouch pockets, the cloak was perfect to wear when running for shelter. You could put all sorts of things in its pockets, from household items to cans of food.

Running for shelter was not a strange thing during wartime. Americans thought they could be attacked at any time. In many places, they did air-raid drills. A siren would sound. People would take cover in safe places. Many built shelters underground. So women wearing kangaroo cloaks—stuffed with goods—would be very popular people in such a shelter!

Don't Be Choosy With Your Shoes!

How high are your heels? In the 1940s, they could not be higher than one inch. That's right. The government limited how high shoes could be.

There also was not a lot of leather for shoes. After all, leather was needed for army boots. Therefore, fashion limited the number of colors for leather shoes to the most popular.

Only six colors of leather were available for shoes. They were mostly neutral in shades of brown and black.

Discover Your Inner Reptile

There may have been a shortage of leather but there was plenty of alligator and snake! These reptile skins were used to make shoes. Sometimes they were used as a trim.

33

No ration stamp required for these smart desk-to-date styles

ENDURA-FLEX SOLES . . . featured on Sears non-rationed women's footwear, are guaranteed to wear as long as leather . . . if not perfectly satisfied your money will be returned. They are either synthetic soles of rubber-like compound . . . plastic coated soles . . . or soles of a strong heavy belting-like material, impregnated with compounds to resist moisture and wear. They have been doubly tested. . . . rigidly tested by Sears own laboratory and wear-tested on hundreds of feet. We know you will be more than satisfied with their long wearing qualities.

"Baby doll" ankle strap in a
premiere appearance

$2.98

This new little number is a real eye catcher with its provocative, new anklet strap and its rounded little girl vamp. Packed with prettiness, it will be seen all around town—from offices to dance-floors, because it's so much fun to wear. You can have these shoes and your stamp, too, because they're non-rationed. You endura-flex soles are specially treated to give resistance to wear and weather.
• C (medium) width in women's sizes 3½ to 9. All half sizes are included, too.

No ration stamp required for these shoes
54 H 7826—Black gabardine . . . 2⅛ inch heels
54 H 7827—Black gabardine . . . 2½ inch heels
State size. Shipping weight . . 1½ pounds.

D'Orsay pump . . . thrillingly beautiful'
. . . truly outstanding

$3.98

Charming salute to a new spring with a flattering version of the D'Orsay . . . its graceful open back, open toe and its saucy little circle bow give it a height of smartness . . . with endura-flex soles . . .

Women did not have to give up rationing stamps for these shoes because they were not made from leather and the soles were specially treated to resist damage from everyday use and weather. The government issued rationing stamps to make sure everyone received his or her fair share of scarce goods. Food, clothes, and shoes were among the many items that were rationed during World War II.

Other times, they were used for the whole shoe. Reptile skins were a bit more expensive, so the woman wearing them would probably be quite well-off.

Learn to Knit

Knitting was a very popular activity in the 1940s. People made their own socks and other items of clothing. There were even knitting patterns for soldiers so they could knit in their spare time! Of course wool yarn was not always available. Sometimes people unraveled old socks or other articles to use the yarn for knitting something completely new!

A model dons a Fair Isle cap and gloves on the front cover of a knitting booklet in 1946. Fair Isle refers to a style of knitting from the Shetland Islands of Scotland that featured bands of colorful geometric designs. Knitting was a necessary skill during the war. It was also a fun way to make unique accessories.

Chapter 6

Pop Culture

On December 7, 1941, the Japanese bombed Pearl Harbor, Hawaii. That was where many of the U.S. military ships were docked. As a result, the United States went to war.

The British and French had already been fighting the war for years. They started back in 1939 when Germany invaded Poland. Germany began taking over more countries. By the time the United States got involved, Germany had conquered Norway, Denmark, Holland, Belgium, France, Yugoslavia, and Greece.

The United States sent soldiers over to Europe and Africa and throughout the Pacific. They would remain there until 1945 when Germany and Japan surrendered. Back in the States, women took over men's jobs to keep the factories and businesses running.

Pop Culture

Between the war, working in factories, and making their own clothes, there was a lot to think about. Americans needed ways to relax and unwind.

Movies were one way to escape the pressure. Such films as *Casablanca* and *Mrs. Miniver* showed courageous wartime stories. They helped people feel hopeful. Sometimes there were short newsreels before the movie that asked for donations for the war and updated audiences on how the Allies were doing. The Allies were the nations fighting against Germany, Italy, and Japan, who were known as the Axis. The United States, England, France, and the Soviet Union were the four big Allied powers, but many other countries sent their soldiers to fight alongside them.

Movie actors and actresses were not just on the screen. A significant number of actors served in the military. Many of them were in combat. Others went overseas to entertain the soldiers. Even if they weren't there, their pictures were. Soldiers often pinned actresses' pictures up on the wall. They became known as pinup girls.

Magazines were not just fun to read but also practical. They offered lots of advice on how to make clothes and reuse items. *Vogue,* a major fashion magazine, had a "Make Do & Mend" program.

Dancing and listening to music were also popular pastimes. Upbeat swing was heard at clubs and dance halls all over the country.

Get the Jitters

When it was time to let off steam, there was the jitterbug. This fast-paced swing dance was so named because dancers looked like they had the jitters. Dancing the jitterbug was done with a partner, moving forward and backward with slides or taps of the feet. Some people got creative. They did turns and even acrobatics.

Swing dancers flip, twist, and spin the night away at the Savoy Ballroom in Harlem, New York, in 1947.

The Pinup Girl

You may not know the name Betty Grable, but chances are that every soldier in World War II did. That was because Betty Grable was on posters in soldiers' lockers and on their walls. Her sexy poses and glamorous look made her a perfect pinup girl.

Pinup girls were not unique to the 1940s. But with soldiers away from home, they were very popular. Actresses and models often posed for the shots, which were then printed for everyone to see.

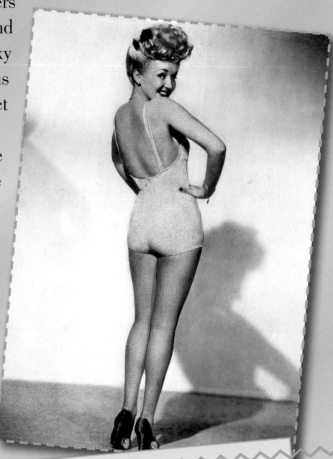

This photograph of American actress Betty Grable (1916–1973) in a bathing suit was the most popular pinup during World War II. Lonely and homesick, soldiers found comfort looking at posters of beautiful women.

Compared to today's photos of actresses and models, the pinup girls were pretty tame. You might see them in a one-piece swimsuit or in a sexy pose, but you would not see a lot of skin.

A Magazine for Teens?

"Young fashions & beauty, movies and music, ideas & people. . . ." So read the cover of the world's first-ever magazine for teenagers, *Seventeen*. Making its first appearance in September 1944, *Seventeen* introduced a groundbreaking idea—teenagers as their own social group. It showed advertisers that they could successfully sell to this group. The actual term *teenager* came later—in the 1950s.

The April 1949 issue of *Seventeen* magazine. *Seventeen* is still popular with teenagers today.

Tupperware

You might have seen those plastic containers called Tupperware®. They were invented in 1942. Earl Tupper was a chemist at DuPont when he saw the new plastic, polyethylene. He thought it was perfect for glasses and bowls, so he made some of his own.

At first, Tupperware was sold in stores. Then Tupper had a great idea. At the time, some products were being sold at home parties. He decided to try selling Tupperware that way.

It was a huge success. There was a Tupperware party in every town. It was a great way to meet neighbors and buy this useful product. Even today, the Tupperware party tradition continues.

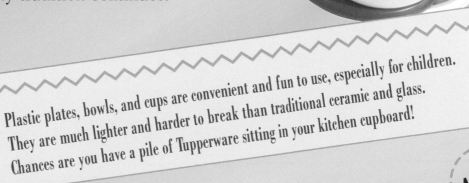

Plastic plates, bowls, and cups are convenient and fun to use, especially for children. They are much lighter and harder to break than traditional ceramic and glass. Chances are you have a pile of Tupperware sitting in your kitchen cupboard!

41

Y Is for Yo-Yo

Do you own a yo-yo? This children's toy was invented in ancient China. Even the ancient Greeks and Romans played with it. But the modern version really came out in the mid-1930s. By the forties, the yo-yo was a household name.

The yo-yo was first produced and sold in the United States by Pedro Flores. His factories reportedly made 300,000 of them a day. The company was taken over by Donald Duncan. He took the yo-yo on the road with trick demonstrations and contests. By 1946, Duncan was making millions of yo-yos a year.

Timeline

The 1920s

The look: cloche hats, dropped-waist dresses, long strands of pearls (women), and baggy pants (men)

The hair: short bobs

The fad: raccoon coats

The 1930s

The look: dropped hemlines, natural waists, practical shoes (women), and blazers and trousers (men)

The hair: finger waves and permanents

The fad: sunbathing

The 1940s

The look: shirtwaist dresses and military style (women) and suits and fedoras (men)

The hair: victory rolls and updos

The fad: kangaroo cloaks

The 1950s

The look: circular skirts and saddle shoes (women) and the greaser look (men)

The hair: bouffants and pompadours

The fad: coonskin caps

The 1960s

The look: bell-bottoms and miniskirts (women) and turtlenecks and hipster pants (men)

The hair: beehives and pageboys

The fad: go-go boots

The 1970s

The look: designer jeans (women) and leisure suits (men)

The hair: shags and Afros

The fad: hot pants

The 1980s

The look: preppy (women and men) and *Miami Vice* (men)

The hair: side ponytails and mullets

The fad: ripped, off-the-shoulder sweatshirts

The 1990s

The look: low-rise, straight-leg jeans (both women and men)

The hair: the "Rachel" cut from *Friends*

The fad: ripped, acid-washed jeans

The 2000s

The look: leggings and long tunic tops (women) and the sophisticated urban look (men)

The hair: feminine, face-framing cuts (with straight hair dominating over curly)

The fad: organic and bamboo clothing

Glossary

accessories—Items that are not part of your main clothing but worn with it, such as jewelry, gloves, hats, and belts.

bobby sox—Ankle socks worn by teenagers; named after the slang term for British police officers.

chignon—A soft bun pinned at the nape of the neck.

dungarees—Blue jeans for women.

fad—A short-term craze.

Fair Isle—A style of knitting that features colorful geometric designs.

fashion—The current style of dressing.

fedora—A wide-brimmed hat pinched at the front.

overalls—A one-piece denim garment made up of a front panel, shoulder straps, and trousers.

raffia—Fibers of an African palm tree; usually made into baskets.

sheath—A simple, mid-length, figure-hugging dress.

trend—The general direction in which things are heading.

turban—A head covering that is a cloth wrapped around the head.

utility—The practical and basic style of clothing in the 1940s due to the shortages of fabric and other materials during wartime.

wedge—A raised shoe of which the heel and sole are part of a solid block.

zoot suit—A suit characterized by a long jacket with wide padded shoulders and baggy trousers cuffed tightly around the ankles.

Further Reading

Books

Baker, Patricia. *Fashions of a Decade: The 1940s.* New York: Facts on File, 2006.

Jones, Jen. *Fashion History: Looking Great Through the Ages.* Mankato, Minn.: Capstone Press, 2007.

Leventon, Melissa. *What People Wore When: A Complete Illustrated History of Costume From Ancient Times to the Nineteenth Century for Every Level of Society.* New York: St. Martin's Griffin, 2008.

Lindop, Edmund, and Margaret J. Goldstein. *America in the 1940s.* Minneapolis, Minn.: Twenty-First Century Books, 2009.

Internet Addresses

Fashion-Era, "1940s Fashion History"
<http://www.fashion-era.com/1940s/index.htm>

The Costume Gallery, "20th Century Fashion Women and Children's Fashions: 1940s"
<http://www.costumegallery.com/1940.htm>

Index

A
Allies, 37
Axis, 37

B
bra, 30, 31

C
chignon, 11

D
Dior, Christian, 14, 18, 19

F
fedora, 22–23

G
Germans, 13, 36, 37

H
Hawaiian shirts, 21–22

J
James, Charles, 19

K
kangaroo cloak, 33
knitting, 27, 32, 35

L
liberty cut, 9, 11

M
McCardell, Claire, 20
military look, 14, 15

N
New Look, 18, 19

O
omelet fold, 11, 12
overalls, 15

P
Paris, France, 13
pinup girl, 37, 39, 40

S
sheath, 14, 16
shirtwaist dress, 15
stockings, 4, 5

T
T-shirt, 22
teenagers, 5, 11, 40
turban, 26, 27, 28

U
utility fashion, 14

V
victory roll, 9, 10, 16
Vivier, Roger, 27

W
wedge, 20, 27, 29, 30

Z
zoot suit, 23–24